Grand Duets for Piano

6 Early Intermediate Pieces for One Piano, Four Hands

Melody Bober

I can still remember performing my very first piano duet. The sound of four hands playing together was amazing. Whether playing with my teacher or a friend, it was always exciting to make music together.

While duets are enjoyable, they also offer a great musical experience for students. Rhythm, phrasing, articulation, and dynamics all become wonderful teaching tools while students learn to listen for that unique blending of parts. I have written *Grand Duets for Piano*, Book 4, so that today's piano students can have as much fun as I did. The duets in this collection contain music in a variety of keys, styles, meters, and tempos designed to help students progress technically and musically...together!

Duets continue to spark excitement in my studio. I sincerely hope that you will enjoy these *Grand Duets for Piano*!

Best wishes,

Melody Bober

CONTENTS

Russian Festival Dance

Secondo

Melody Bober

Russian Festival Dance

Primo

Melody Bober

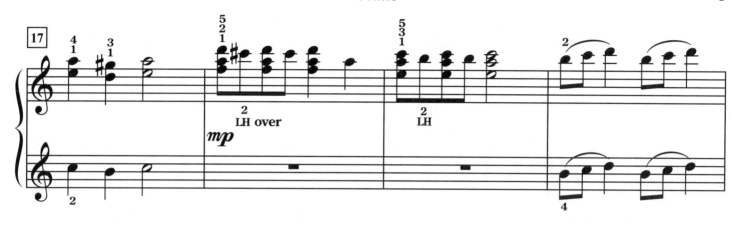

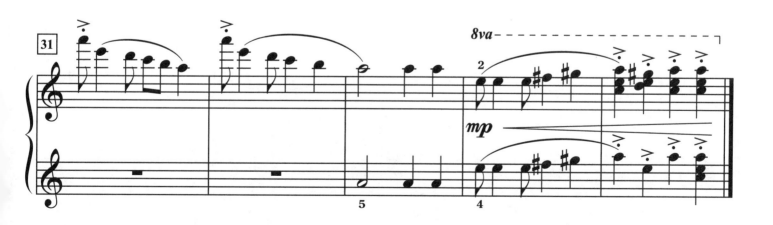

Fiesta Fun

Secondo

Melody Bober

Fiesta Fun

Primo

Melody Bober

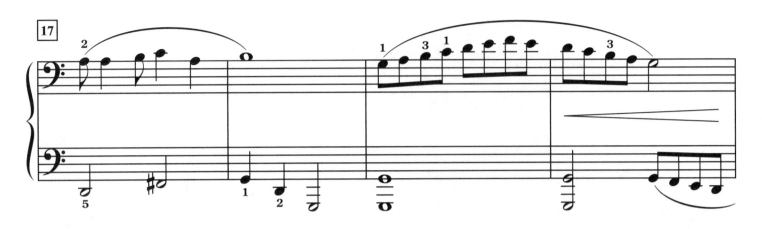

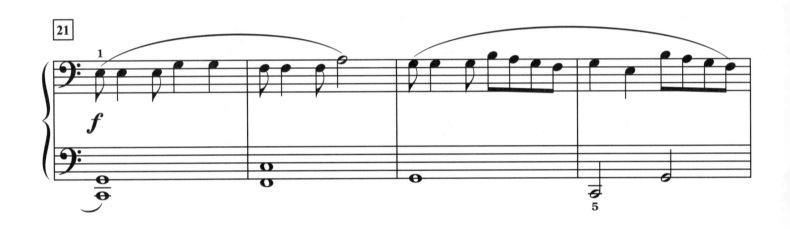

A Mysterious Moment

Secondo

Melody Bober

A Mysterious Moment

Primo

Melody Bober

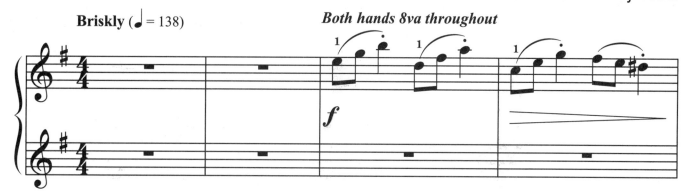
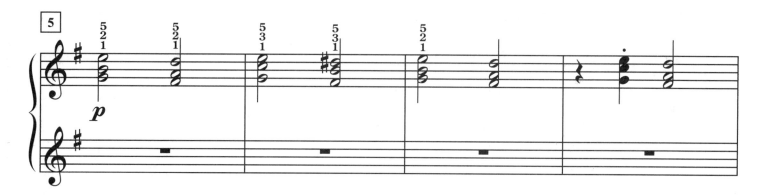

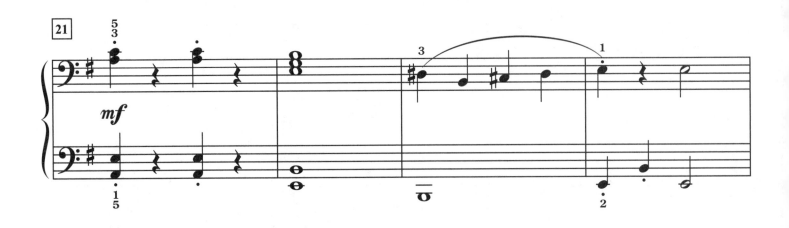

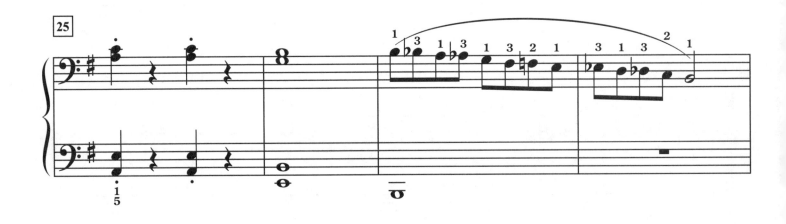

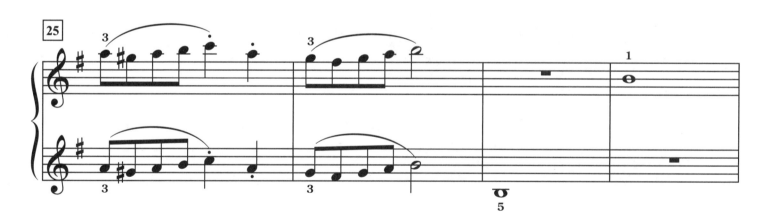

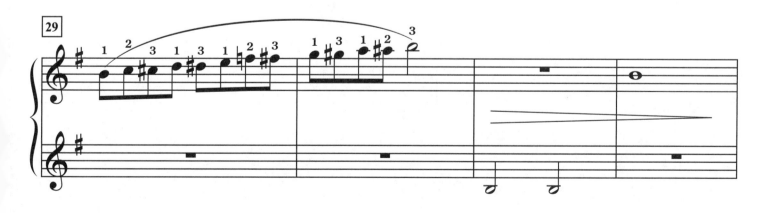

Secondo

Nostalgia

Secondo

Melody Bober

Nostalgia

Primo

Melody Bober

Secondo

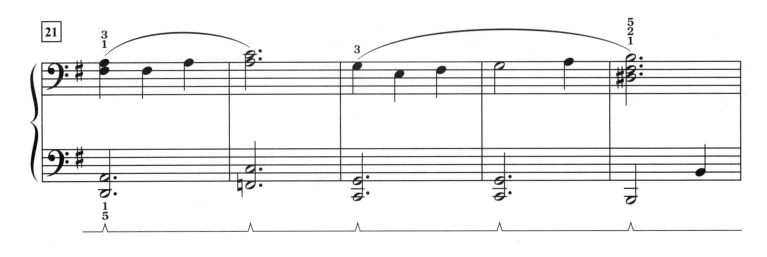

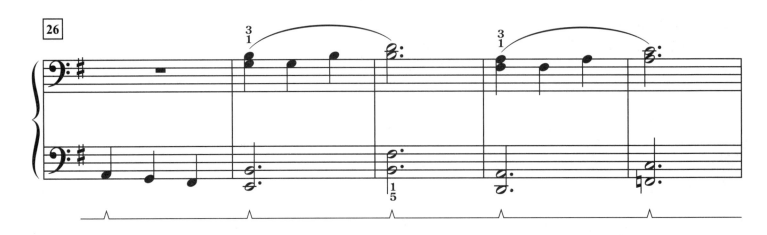

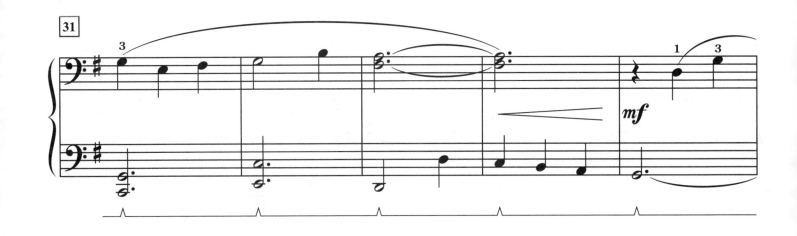

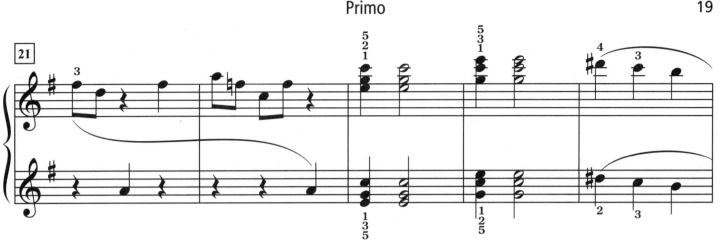

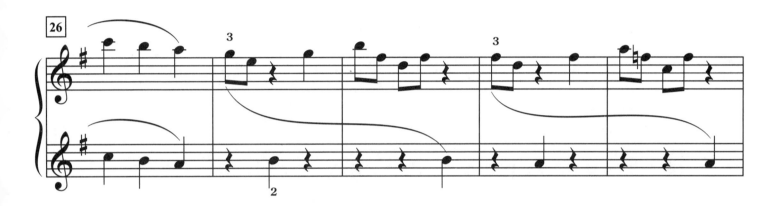

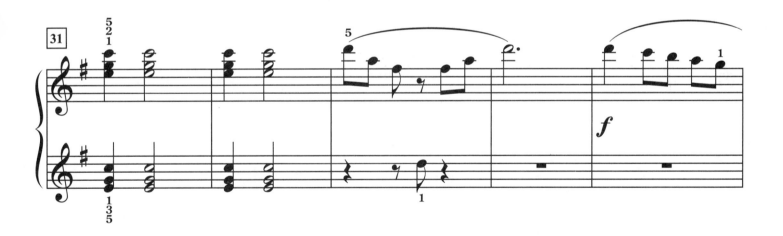

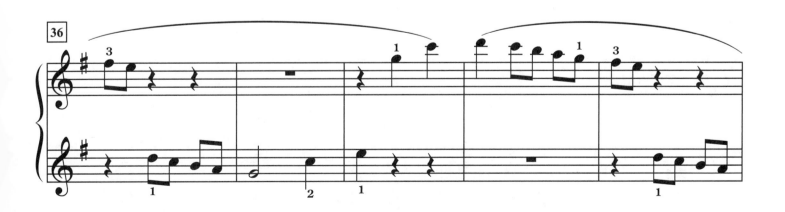

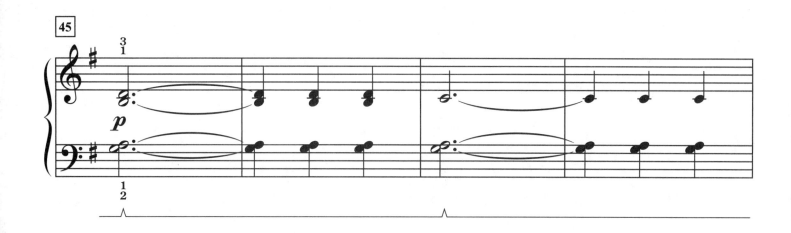

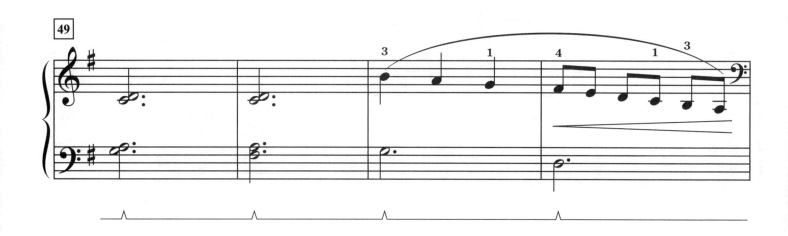

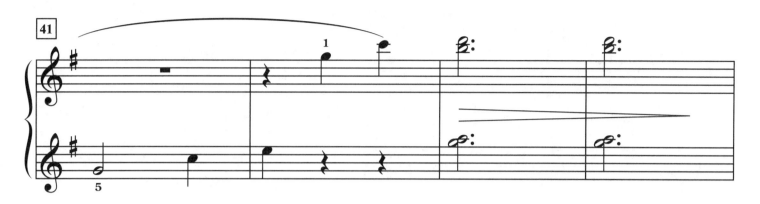

Both hands 8va to the end

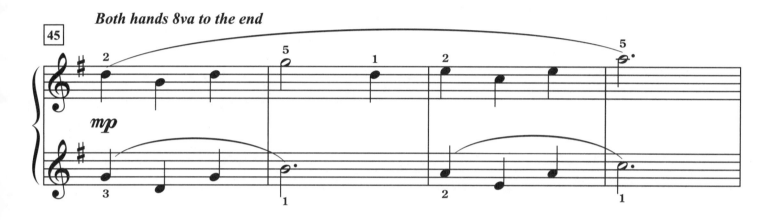

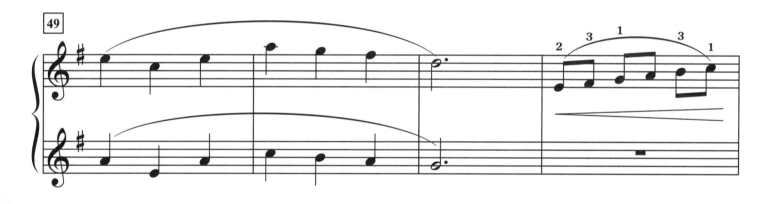

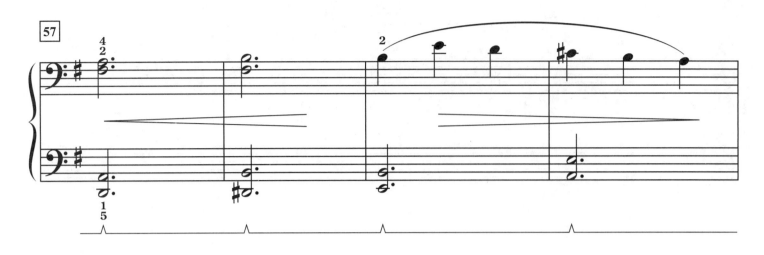

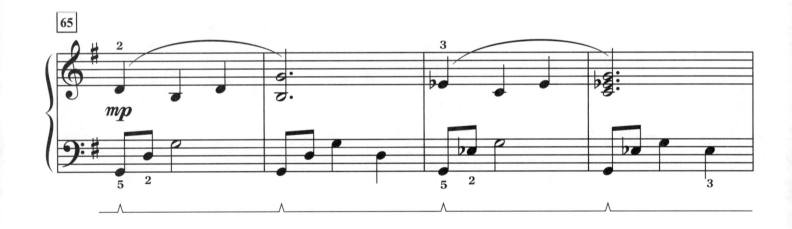

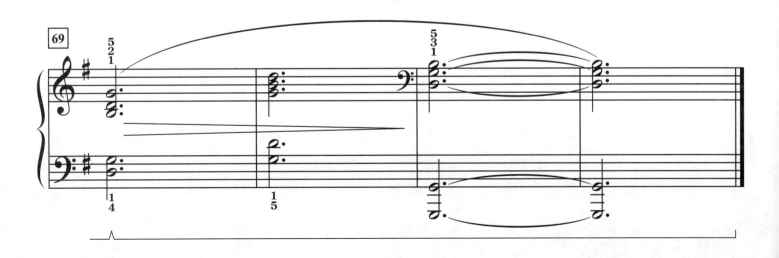

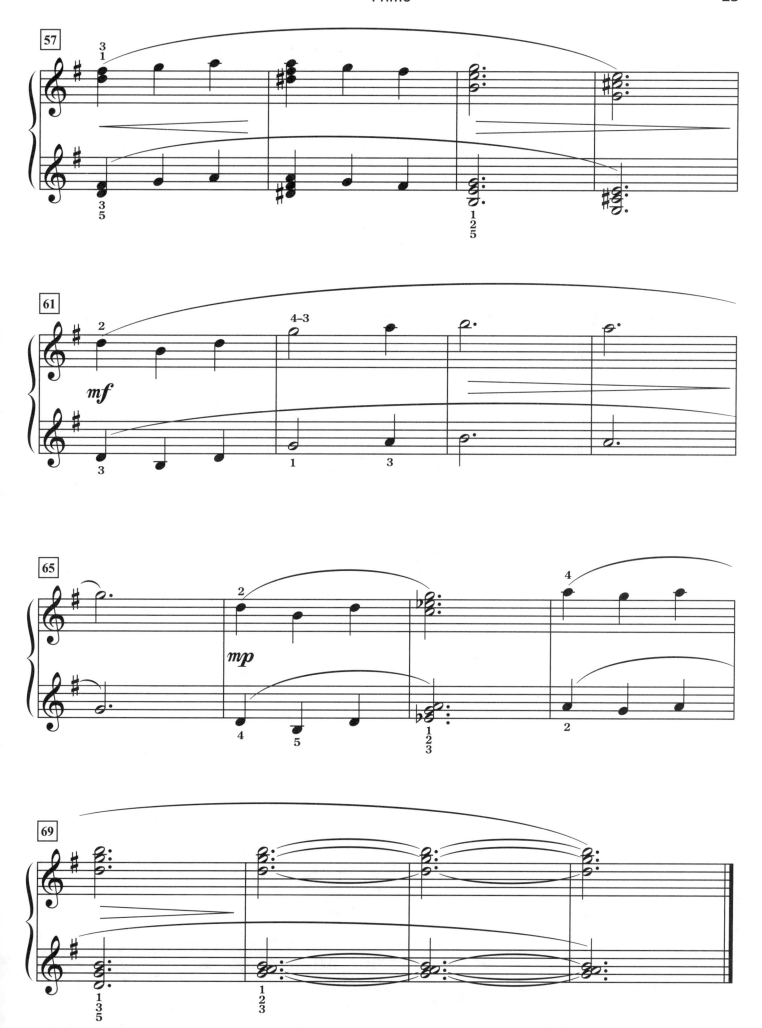

Rock Solid

Secondo

Melody Bober

Rock Solid

Primo

Melody Bober

Ancient Legend

Secondo

Melody Bober

Ancient Legend

Primo

Reflective (♩ = 92)

Melody Bober

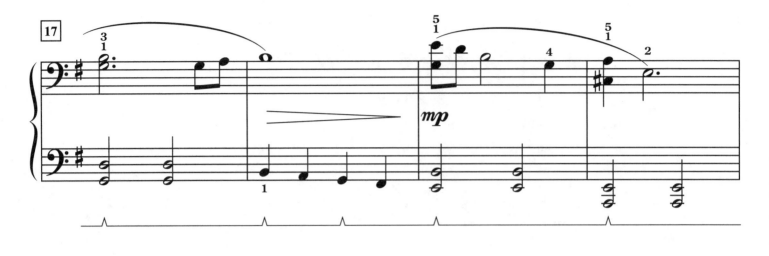

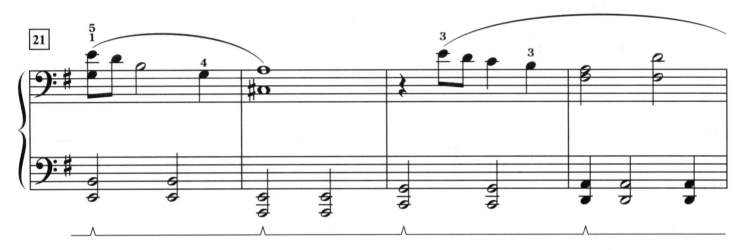

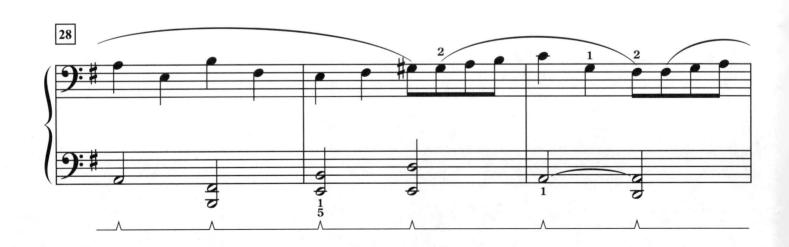

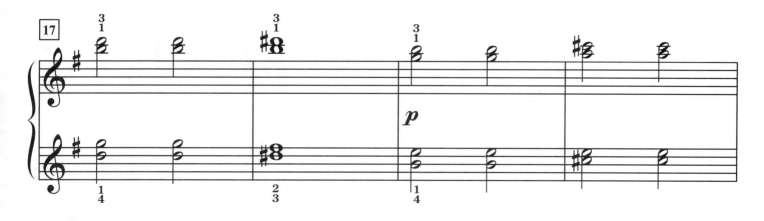

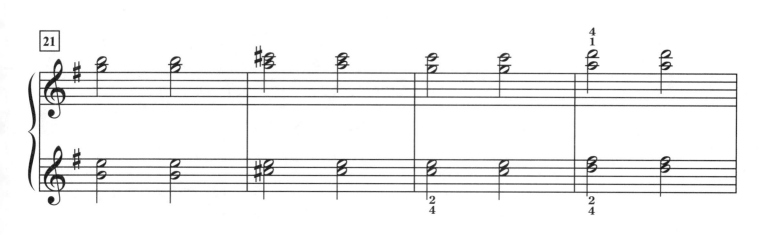

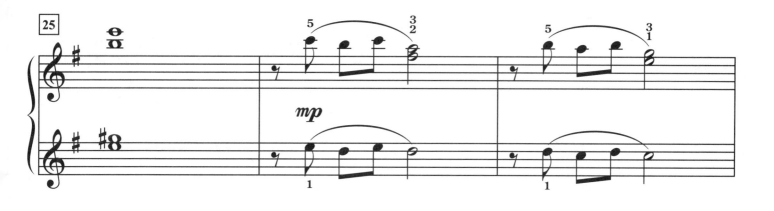

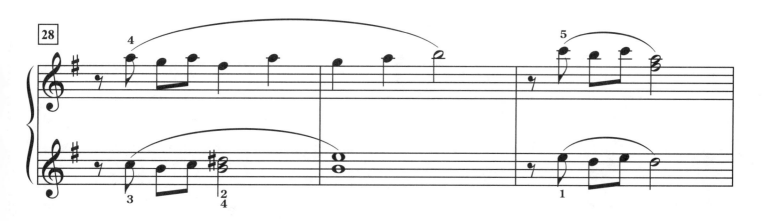

Secondo

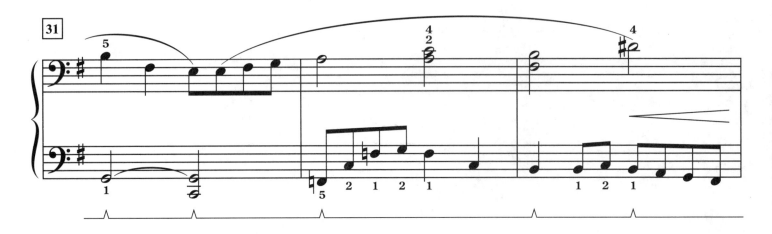

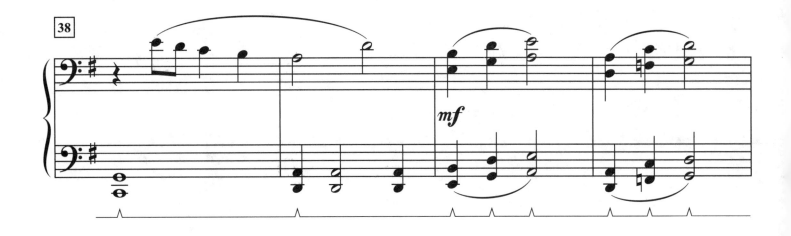

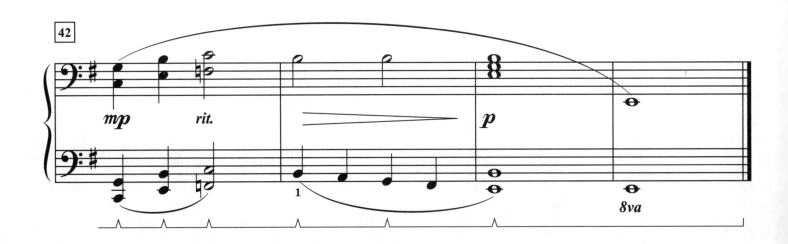

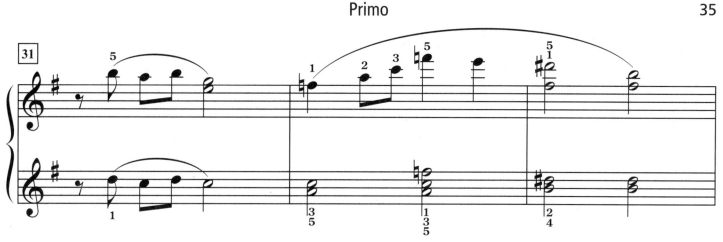

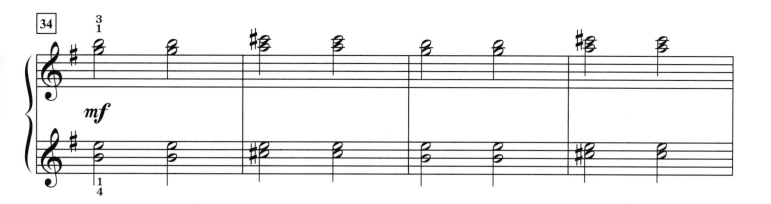

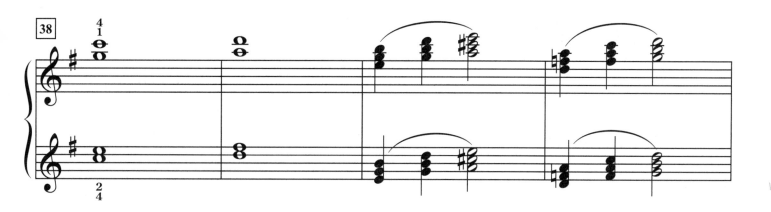

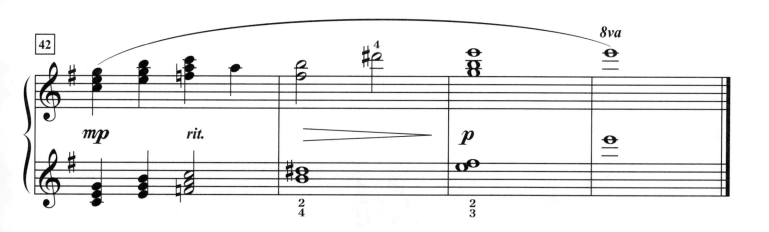